FLOW

From Pure and Safe Water to Higher States of Consciousness

Patrick Durkin

I0005539

BEYOND
B E L I E F
—PUBLISHING—
YOU HOLD THE FUTURE IN YOUR HANDS

ISBN: 978-1-945446-91-7

I dedicate this book to coherence within the human species, such that we choose love, joy, and harmony.

Contents

Acknowledgments

This book is offered in gratitude to those who dare speak their truth in the face of disagreement. Thank you to pioneers and water scientists including Viktor Schauberger, Dr. Masaru Emoto, Konstantin Korotkov, Gerald Pollack, and Gina Bria.

Thank you to the courageous chiropractors, acupuncturists, energy workers, Reiki healers, yoga teachers, astrologers, hydrotherapists, functional medicine practitioners, homeopaths, reflexologists, energetic alchemists, and alternative health providers from all walks of life.

Thank you to all our customers around the world who are immersing themselves in structured water.

Thank you to those who have supported The Wellness Enterprise, Inc. to become a reality, including David Kujawa, Ryan Andrews, Holland Franklin, Chad Wall, Maryellen Smith, Arttemis Keszainn, Nikki Jencen, Valerie Valencia, Susanna Thomas, and many friends and colleagues at CEO Space International.

Thank you to my children, Amanda, Peter, James, and Emily, who endured years of experiments and unending conversations about water.

And, a special thanks to Jennifer Lee Solin, who has immersed herself in The Wellness Enterprise and loved me and our customers just the way we are.

Introduction

In 2007, I watched the documentary *An Inconvenient Truth* and came across a lot of headlines about global warming. I became acutely aware that there is a need for change in our world.

This book is about a surprising journey that shocked me in its complexity, depth, magic, and multi-dimensional nature. It began as a community service project to get rid of plastic water bottles and wound its way into local schools—where I inspired students to learn about hydration and environmental awareness—then it morphed into understanding water quality, filtration, and purification. I was so intrigued that I started a full, personal investigation of filtration. I was surprised to see how complex the world of water filtration is!

I wrote this book because so many people don't feel safe or confident about the quality of their water. I wrote it because people don't understand the energy of water. And I wrote the book because people are living with the illusion of being separate. I want everybody to have the opportunity to live from a perspective of connectedness because it is a much more satisfying and fulfilling way to live.

The big revelation is that the whole conversation about water filters has been driven by fear, teaching people to remove things from their water. This is worth studying, because from my perspective, there is a philosophical conflict here. I view the world through the perspective of oneness, which means there's no such thing as *over there, throwing away,* or *removing.* From that perspective, I can't remove anything from my water.

I feel like I've reached a point of understanding in which the gifts I have received and the magic I have witnessed have been so deep that I can't go any further without stopping and recording this aspect of the journey in a book to share with you, so you can consider getting rid of plastic water bottles and becoming aware that water is the path to world peace. My journey has been so deep that I've created a course called "Water Magic 101" to share what I've learned. I still feel that the journey to understanding water is infinitely deep, and I will never finish.

CHAPTER ONE

The Journey Begins

TRANSFORMATION

I have always thought of myself as somebody who is constantly improving his life. By *improvement*, I mean I'm a little bit more capable, a little bit deeper, and see a broader perspective and experience more each month, season, and year of my life. Recently, I've found something way more stimulating and exciting than improvement: *transformation*.

What does transformation mean to me?

Say I'm approaching an area of my life in which I want to expand. Rather than improving, the entire area transforms into something I wasn't even thinking about at the beginning. That's what transformation is to me, and that's what this journey with water has been about.

Why Doesn't Achieving the American Dream Feel Good?

A significant portion of my life has been defined by the schooling that I've gone through, the media stories that I've read, the way people talk to one another, the way institutions, organizations, and even family are aligned and created. They're structures. Inside of what I learned from those structures, I took the training to mean that I should compete for money; that there was an amount that I should go after for my family, so that we would be better off. I lived with an illusion that I was going to feel good if I gained something called the *American Dream*. It says you can achieve your dream, create something, get rich, and then everything is going to be better. The thing is, at the ripe old age of thirty, I had already won the American Dream. I made a million dollars that year, and every morning, I still woke up with fear in my heart, deteriorating health, and an overall sense of unworthiness.

Appearances Can Be Deceiving

On the outside, my life probably looked pretty good. For my thirty-fifth birthday, I bought myself a Porsche, and as if that wasn't enough, I put my initials on the license plate. I remodeled a huge home across the street from the ocean. I had a family with four kids. *Success!* is what it looked like on the outside.

Ha! is how it felt inside.

I was an emotional and physical wreck. I had daily pain in my joints. My emotions were often a train wreck. I was sacrificing my health in service of earning more money for my family. So, while people might have seen me driving my ten-minute commute across town in a Porsche and think that things were going well, the truth is that my heart knew fear.

This Is *So* Boring

I don't know if you can imagine what it was like to be me, listening to the thoughts in my head, but let me see if I can describe it to you.

It was *so* boring!

My thoughts were focused on a limited scope:

- Making money
- Sports
- Beer
- Competition

If I went to a cocktail party or met someone noteworthy, those are the people and events I talked about. I'd meet people who were interested in different things, passionate about different areas of life, and I would offer no contribution to the conversation if it wasn't about the financial markets, the Patriots, or the Red Sox. It was horrible!

I stayed up at night, praying to life, like: *Please let me lead a more interesting life. Please let me be interested in and talk about something other than these boring topics.*

That's when something interesting happened.

I attended a course with my business partners that was designed to help each of us focus our attention on what we wanted for our lives. One exercise asked us to draw our visions.

My business partners' visions were the visions of financial advisors:

- They wanted to make a lot of money.

- They wanted to network with accountants and attorneys.

- They wanted to lead a traditional life based on selling financial services.

My vision board was covered. I drew a little vehicle with a light shining out on the world, and waterfalls, birds, and greenhouses on top of houses. What it meant to me was there was a revolution going on in our systems and our ways of thinking, and I wanted to be part of an environmental cause, a change-of-consciousness cause, something to make life more interesting.

That course opened the doorway to intense change.

MOTHER EARTH IS CALLING

By the time the documentary *An Inconvenient Truth* came out (2006), I had already positioned myself with deepening interests in environmental causes. I was the chairman of the recycling committee in my town, and I found that I had a lot of passion for understanding recycling.

When we extract resources, use them, and discard them, where do they go?

As this movement for becoming aware of global warming, of humans' connection to the environment, was taking hold, I was in a position to do some experimenting and hear the call of Mother Earth.

Trash Gyres

As chairman of the recycling committee, I could engage and act locally while learning about global issues. The great Pacific trash gyre, which is reportedly larger than the state of Texas, is in the Pacific Ocean. It's a place where the plastics that we carelessly let roll off our land are brought together by wind and current into a large floating island of debris. So, imagine something larger than Texas, made up of degrading plastic in the water column. The fish confuse plastic debris with their food sources and feed off it. The birds living there fill their bellies with plastic, to the point that they can no longer digest. When their carcasses are examined, their digestive tracts are found clogged with plastic waste.

Our lifestyle is based on illusions that have been marketed to us, including the ideas that convenience is important—more important than anything—and that there's such a thing as throwing something away. There are now six trash gyres—six places where all this waste from humans aggregates in our oceans. I started to understand that our choices about what we do on a daily basis impact the whole. If fish ingest plastic and we ingest the fish, we're going to end up being humans with plastic toxins in our bodies. In fact, I recently revisited my research on this topic. What I found is that some recent water testing was done, and 83 percent of water tested around the world was found to contain microplastics. So not only the fish are damaged; now we are too.[1]

A Project Within the Bureaucracy

Once I heard the call from Mother Earth for humans to become more responsible as a species, I knew that there was something within my power to do in my town. I led our recycling committee to recycle infrastructure all over town. We focused on some of the most public locations—high-visibility street corners, municipal buildings, the library, the schools—and we provided recycling bins.

I thought this type of project would be fairly easy. The truth is it took two years because of all the red tape. As we completed

---

1 *The Guardian.* theguardian.com/environment/2017/sep/06/plastic-fibres-found-tap-water-around-world-study-reveals

the project, I realized that what we had done didn't scale as a solution to the problems that I was focused on. In other words, Mother Earth was not calling for an improvement; and recycling was an improvement type of project. Mother Earth was calling for transformation—was calling for us to not use plastic bottles, not direct waste into our oceans. If that was going to happen, we had to make changes at a much faster and stronger gradient than just providing recycling bins.

Heartbreak

Right after we finished the project of putting the bins in, I went for a ride around town and looked at our work. I had the strangest feeling. It was hard for me to identify. It took me weeks to know what to call it. When I could finally identify it, I knew it was *heartbreak*. I felt sad. My sadness was about the feeling that I had given people a reason to feel better about using a plastic water bottle and putting it in a recycling bin, as if that was some sort of solution that was going to help Mother Earth. But inside, I knew that it wasn't helping at all.

I formed a new idea. My new idea was to start a transformational project. Instead of giving people little solutions, I wanted to give them something that would change the way they think, so that they would never again use a plastic water bottle. It's as if we were treating only the symptoms of the problem, and I wanted to discover the root cause. I called the new project, designed to create this transformational change in the world, *Water Works*.

WATER WORKS: TRANSFORMATION IN MOTION

By now, you're probably starting to understand that I want to make a difference in changing my own life, the lives of people around me who are interested, and the interaction between our species and the Earth.

Passion for Change

No problem can be solved from the same level of consciousness that created it.

~ attributed to Albert Einstein

The passion that I felt to create a transformational service project was fuel for my body, mind, and soul. In fact, it was enough to cause me to end my career as a financial advisor.

One day I was talking with my mom, and she said, "You seem to be more passionate about your plastic water bottle project than you are with managing my money. What's going on over there?"

Between the course that I had been to with my business partners and what my mom was saying, I realized that life was tapping me on the shoulder and saying, "It's time to move on. It's time to shift your vocation to something that you feel more passionate about."

I left my career as a financial advisor and set out to change our level of consciousness about water so we can create an entirely new system.

As I looked further into the issue, I noticed that people don't feel safe about water. They don't feel confident about water quality, and that's why they use plastic bottles. That realization drove me to a deep inquiry into the different types of water and plastic bottles and ultimately into water filters as well.

Marketplace Matching: Products and People

I knew that if I were going to help transform our consciousness about water, I had to share with people a story that was so powerful that they would stop their current behaviors, and they would shift to this new story. So, fueled by that passion, I began to engage with people just like you.

I asked people, "How do you treat your water? What type of filters do you use? Do you use a water pitcher, an under-sink filter, a countertop filter, maybe an alkaline water machine, or a water cooler?"

I ended up selling all these types of devices, and exploring the reactions that people had to them. I even found vending machines that filtered water inside the machine so that you could fill your own reusable container with it. I found a vending machine that filtered water and even made alkaline water!

As I continued in this line of inquiry, I could feel that people wanted me to succeed in finding a solution for the plastic water bottle problem. So, I kept going.

I met with many different entities, including:

- Superintendents of school districts
- Corporate headquarters for the Gap in San Francisco
- Town managers
- Water companies

I had to know which water treatment system would cause people to change their behavior on the spot.

A Vision Without a Plan

I sense many people hold a deep desire for world peace. I have long desired this as well but when I look under "World Leaders" in my Rolodex, glance at my speed dial, or scroll through my contacts, I simply didn't see any.

I began asking myself, "How can I make an impact on a global basis?" and realized that I better start looking somewhere else.

I wondered: *What can I do inside my own being and then radiate outward to the beings I influence? Then, maybe because I'm so strong at radiating it, it will go through them out to the beings that they influence. Maybe I could contribute to world peace by changing myself.*

I always found that empowering.

I see the plastic water bottle problem as being connected to world peace because it's connected to the way we think:

- Who we think we are
- What we think the Earth is
- What the relationship is between our species and our planet

Inside of that type of thinking, I formed a vision. My vision is that everyone receives a new message that the impact of delivering plastic water bottles to the shelves where we buy them, and the quality of the water within them, is harmful to the Earth and the people, such that we never want to buy those bottles again.

My vision is that all the bottles on the shelves of all the places that sell plastic water bottles right now stay there. They stay there for long enough so when the next delivery comes, the boxes stack up, and there's no room to unload the bottles onto the shelves. Then, the next time the delivery comes and there's no room for the boxes, the truck goes back to the factory with the bottles still on the truck. Then, there's no room on the trucks, so the factory doesn't load anymore on trucks. Then, there's no reason to take any more water out of the ground, and we just leave our water where it is.

That's my vision. I hadn't yet imagined a clear plan for how it was going to happen. But I had an unrelenting passion for asking the questions that would reveal the story to me.

> *The water is so wonderful; it feels so alive when I take a sip from it. It's as though I can feel and sense beautiful crystals on my lips, tongue, and roof of my mouth. I never expected there to be such a contrast between the water I usually drink and the structured water.*
>
> ~ Donna

CHAPTER TWO

The Living Water Movement

STRUCTURED WATER

The human body functions optimally when given a steady supply of living foods and living water.

A Promising Discovery

After several years matching people and products, I'd become knowledgeable about traditional water filters, and I still wasn't satisfied with the solutions I was offering people. Most of my customers were happy with the products I shared with them, but none of them were excited. I was still looking for *the* solution to the water problem. Then, I bumped into a friend at a conference.

I told him about my discoveries with water filters, and he asked me why I was only treating water with chemistry instead of physics.

I said, "What do you mean?"

He said, "You know about structured water, don't you?"

When I replied no, he smiled, laughed, and said, "Oh boy, you're going to love this!"

He explained that structuring water increases the energy in water, which increases the energy in everything, like people and plants. I was intrigued. Everybody wants more energy, and if they could find it in water, that would surely be a big hit. This idea seemed like it would scale to the size of the problems I was trying to solve.

As I researched structured water, I was particularly interested in the benefits of increased energy. I knew if my customers could feel an increase in energy from using my products, then anything was possible.

Structured Water Is the Type of Water Found in Nature

Water found in fruits and vegetables, springs, mountain streams, and rain is structured water. It is also the water found in the cells of living things, including us! New physics and wave particle knowledge shows us that when water moves and spins, it re-organizes and re-structures to create electrical charge.

Once this change happens, water is better described as structured water. Structured water describes what water does in motion, over space and time. Structuring water allows an electrical charge to begin cascading or hopping from one molecule to another, creating more charge, more energy. The spin and structure turn water molecules into tiny batteries. Though theorized for over one hundred years, it was first documented by Dr. Gerald Pollack at the Pollack Lab, University of Washington, Seattle.

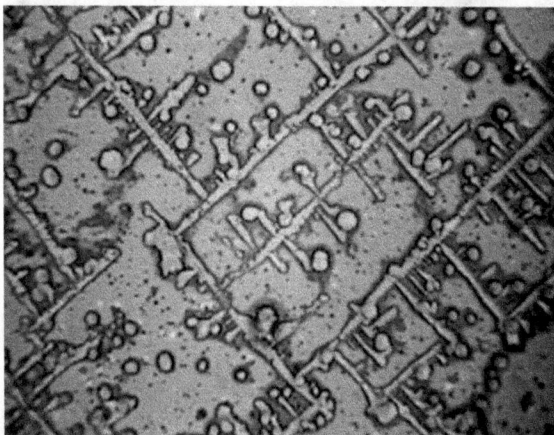

Image caption: Sample of neutral tap water from Bottighofen, Switzerland. The 90-degree angular structures represent toxic substances.

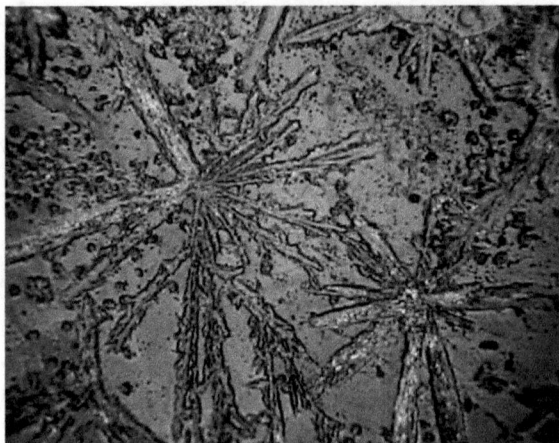

Image caption: Structured sample of Bottighofen tap water processed with a Natural Action water structuring device. Note the absence of 90-degree structures, indicating the structured sample is free of toxic substances.

Images from "Crystallization Analysis: Quality of Water from Water Purification United Evaluation." Hagalis AG. Naturalaction.info/structured-water.

When I was doing my research, there wasn't one comprehensive website to learn about structured water, but today, you can visit hydrationfoundation.org for your educational needs regarding structured water and its vital role to achieve real hydration.

> *The beauty of a living thing is not the atoms that go into it, but the way those atoms are put together.*
>
> ~ Carl Sagan

Consider diamonds and graphite. They're both made of carbon, and yet they have very different properties. On the one hand, graphite is soft, and on the other, diamonds are hard and shiny. So even though they have the same chemistry, the two of them have different properties. The same is true for water.

You have a choice. You can drink H_2O—hydrogen and oxygen—and have that be ordinary, lifeless water, or you can drink structured water, which is H_3O_2 and is an energized elixir, designed to support your highest physical, mental, and spiritual function.

Which would you choose?

As I came to understand that not all water is simply H_2O, I began looking at this issue from different angles, such as the business model. One of the reasons that we have so much waste in the world is that corporate profits require it. They have a concept called *planned obsolescence*, where they engineer an item to be thrown away, so we'll have to buy another one. It's not that consumer goods can't be engineered to last; it's that they're engineered to be replaced.

This principle applies to water filters too. When I researched further into structured water, I understood that not only was the quality of the product completely different from anything I was used to, the actual products were completely different. They had no replacement parts and no maintenance.

The environmentalist in me was jumping up and down, but the businessman inside of me was saying: *Run away! Run away fast! You don't want to be in a business that doesn't have replacement parts or maintenance. You'll have to find new customers all the time, and that's quite a burden for a business.*

An Experiment

The promise of increased energy and no waste was too good to pass up. I had already experienced a career as a financial advisor that was all about money. I needed to take a leap of faith. The universe was already showing me: When I tried to sell filters, I ended up with clients who were slightly happy, but not elated. The flow of revenue wasn't that good.

What if I could distribute a product that could energize people, hydrate them, and eliminate environmental waste and unnecessary spending?

The prospects were too good to ignore, so I had to find out more.

I decided to try an experiment. After all, the idea of changing the energy of water was definitely not mainstream. At that time, I didn't even know how to talk about it. But I did have some pretty weird friends, so I decided to give some of them a call.

The way the typical call went was like this:

Hi, it's Patrick. I have a new water thing, or thingy, maybe it's called? I'm not really sure what to say about it, but they say it changes the energy of water, it lasts forever, and it makes a big difference for a lot of people in their bodies. Well, I really can't explain it. Could you just go inward for a minute and ask if you're supposed to be one of the people to own one of these devices?

Then I waited, sure that my friends would turn me down. Much to my surprise, I had 11 friends who were willing to buy one of those devices based on that presentation. I considered myself lucky and placed my order, determined not to let bias influence my results. I was going to ship them their devices and wait to hear what they had to say to me.

WATER AS CONSCIOUSNESS

> *Water may be the most malleable computer.*
> ~ Rustum Roy, Material Scientist

As I opened myself up to the possibilities of structured water, I learned from those who came before me, as well as from personal experience. It was important that I be open to learning in different ways because the ideas I've put together are not mainstream. Yet, there are many aspects of them that are well regarded and respected in scientific and educational communities.

Dr. Masaru Emoto

One of the most important water scientists was the late Dr. Masaru Emoto. He tested his hypothesis about water as a living consciousness by exposing water to words and sounds and then freezing the water. He then photographed the ice formations that resulted and compared them. His discoveries and photographs, which have been seen by millions in his *New York Times* best-seller, *The Hidden Messages in Water*, demonstrate the impact of vibration on water (Beyond Words Publishing, 2004).

Vibrations were expressed in his experiments through words and music. He used words, such as *Love* and *Gratitude,* and music, like Mozart. He also contrasted this expression with words, such as *Hate* and *War,* and heavy metal music. What he discovered and photographed is that the vibrations of the words or the music caused the water to form crystals, either extraordinarily beautiful ones or malformed, ugly ones. It was an amazing discovery and opened a door through which many have passed.

There are now Russian scientists who have taken this to the next level, and they're exploring the impact of electromagnetic frequencies on DNA. Others—such as the renowned researcher Gregg Braden, who bridges science and spirituality in his workshops—have shown how sound can be used to raise vibrations and to create increasingly complex sacred geometric shapes.

As science continues to be discovered, I am most interested in the impact on our lives. I've witnessed science in my lifetime that matters only in the laboratory. I search for discoveries to be applicable in our daily lives so our lives are better.

Infinity Wave

Of my 11 friends who purchased structured water devices based on that informal presentation, one is Hope Fitzgerald from the Wave Energy Center for Conscious Evolution. Not long after she received her unit, she invited me to attend a workshop on co-creating with the energy of water as a partner in our lives.

Naturally, I was intrigued and attended the workshop with 11 other participants. I did not go with my business interests in mind; I went as a participant. During our lunch break, Hope brought out her structured water device and shared the impact it had on her health and life. She was using well water, and she absolutely loved the way the structuring device energized her water and made her feel.

Much to my surprise, five of the 11 participants purchased structured water devices from me that day. Simultaneously, the Universe sent me messages through the workshop about the energy of water. It showed me that when people — particularly those who are open-minded and interested in subtle energies — are exposed to structured water devices, they are intrigued enough for nearly 50 percent to purchase them at a weekend workshop.

During the time I was learning about the physical aspects of structured water devices, Hope was receiving spiritual information about a wall of water coming and hitting the planet through her explorations as a gifted dowser and channel for information from the cosmos. She simply didn't know what to make of this but was being instructed to begin hosting workshops.

Hope answered: *Okay, I'll do the workshop, but what am I teaching?*

As the date for the workshop got closer, she was given more and more information.

She kept telling me, "Patrick, you have to come out here and experience this infinity wave workshop!"

I heard the enthusiasm in her voice and understood that I was supposed to be there, but each time I planned to attend, something blocked me. It was like the timing was not in sync.

Eventually, about four months after Hope began using her structured water device, timing finally came into alignment. I attended the workshop, and during the first morning, she asked us to explore visualization exercises. After, she asked for participation from the workshop attendees.

I raised my hand and said, "Hope, when I closed my eyes to visualize, I saw black. There's nothing there."

One of the primary benefits I've experienced with structured water is an extraordinary expansion in my creativity, but in this first attempt, I fell short.

As the infinity wave workshop continued, I became *inhabited*—that's one way of saying it. I received a message from the energy of water. I became aware of a living energy inside me, and I began to practice some of the exercises from the workshop in my daily life.

For instance, as I experienced conflict or resistance in my relationships, I would picture the shape of the infinity sign as a wall of water. I would visualize the infinity wave going back and forth between my heart and the other person's, or I would put the whole wave over their body so they were completely immersed by it. As I visualized this energy of water, things would change. I came to a different understanding than my traditional thinking would have normally created. It was a great delight for me to experience working with both the energy of water and the physical structured water devices at the same time in this way.

Talking With Water

When I was leaving the workshop, Hope gave me a homework assignment, which I promptly forgot (probably because it was a bit advanced for where I was at the time).

A little while later, I remembered the assignment when an issue popped up while I was working from home. I decided to go for a walk along the beach, and as I did so, I remembered what Hope had suggested: talk with water—whatever that meant. There I was, contemplating this issue and Hope's assignment while looking at the ocean waves.

As I framed the question that I wanted to resolve, I looked up at the ocean and thought to myself: *Okay, we're supposed to be talking, so what do you have to say?*

Right before my eyes, a wave started breaking from both ends of the beach, and it met in the middle. I gave an out-loud chuckle and spoke, "Oh, so I'm supposed to take the middle ground with this, is that right?" I laughed and knew that I had just experienced my first interaction—conscious interaction, anyway—of talking with water.

Little did I know how much that practice was going to progress over the coming months and years. I then developed methods of balancing my chakras at the edge of the ocean using long-tone vowel sounds.

I went to another workshop where I met up with a former online business partner. When we were wrapping up the four-day workshop, she understood how much I was communing with the workshop. She said, "Well, it was nice to meet you, and your *wife,* water. I'll see the two of you around sometime!"

I walked away with a hearty chuckle, knowing that people were beginning to notice how much I was embodying the energy, excitement, and inspiration of the structured water movement.

INFINITE ENERGY

In a world ruled by the five senses, we unwittingly constrict ourselves by limiting our perceptions to those senses. I loved that I was learning about and being exposed to infinite energies. When I was in the presence of them, I felt like anything was possible for my life.

Sacred Geometry and the Vortex

At this time in my journey of understanding structured water, I gained a real advantage. I became visible to the public. I was beginning to be interviewed to share my knowledge about structured water. When people heard me, some listeners were more knowledgeable about the topic than I was, and they were generous. I received various phone calls and emails from people who had advanced understandings about water, who wanted me to be more knowledgeable about the topic.

One of those people contacted me to teach me about sacred geometry. She could tell I hadn't yet mastered the topic of infinite energies, and that I didn't really understand what sacred geometry was. Since it was a lifelong passion of hers, she wanted to help.

What she taught me—and what I've been able to see and understand from other sources too—is that sacred geometry is the language of creation. If you've ever walked along the beach and pick up a whorled shell, you may have noticed a spiral in the structure of the shell. The spiral, also referenced in the *Golden Ratio* or the *Fibonacci Sequence,* is a specific mathematical relationship that we can also see in the growth patterns of pine cones and florets in a head of Romanesco broccoli, as well as in the shape of hurricanes and our galaxy.

Another aspect of sacred geometry includes self-similar patterns that repeat on a progressively smaller or larger scale. Known as *fractals*, examples in nature can be seen in snowflakes and other crystals, ferns, lightning bolts, watersheds, and the shorelines of continents. Sacred Geometry is essentially the underlying construct of how things are created in the cosmos. It's an infinite energy; it carries the energy of creating.

Simultaneously, she also taught me about the Vortex. A vortex is something that spins infinitely fast. That means if a mathematician tries to explain a vortex to us, they would tell us that the spin inside the vortex is faster than we can label; we can't understand it. Vortexes can be seen in the shape of a tornado, or as I've come to realize, there are actually vortexes in the water at the ocean. There's an infinite number of them.

I discovered this by going for walks in the water about thigh deep. I noticed that as I walked, water spun off each of my legs into vortexes. I was amused by being surrounded by these infinite energies. As I was learning about these concepts in nature, I was coming to understand that these same infinite energies were the ones that were propelling the technology inside structured water devices.

Hydrogen Bond Angles

As delighted as I was about the exploration of the infinite energies through sacred geometry and vortexes, I needed hardcore science too. Fortunately, there are a lot of discoveries happening right now in the structured water field.

The origin of the industry is attributed to Viktor Schauberger, an Austrian naturalist who discovered that he could move logs downstream more easily if the logs were spinning and the river was curving. There have been a lot of discoveries since then, probably none more impactful than the laboratory report on hydrogen bond angles from the German lab, Hagalis AG.

The Hagalis AG lab reports show that when water is subjected to infinite energies like sacred geometry and vortexes, the way the hydrogen and the oxygen are bonded together changes. This is much like the changes we talked about earlier, where graphite and diamonds are both made of the same chemistry—carbon—but have very different properties. The Hagalis AG report shows that the hydrogen bond angles expand and, in so doing, change the properties of the water.[2]

This change is how we can have water that energizes people more, that causes plants to grow better, that essentially causes people to reset their biological systems back into alignment with the way they were designed. It's an important report, and it's one that I was pleased to find because it helped ground what I was studying and seeing in my own life.

---

2 Schulz, Andreas. "Crystallization Analysis: Quality of Water from Water Purification Units Evaluation." Hagalis AG. 31zet510utp2pcr5bx3zzqen-wpengine.netdna-ssl.com/wp-content/uploads/2014/08/German-Scientific-Structured-Water-Test-Results-2012.pdf

"I Like Water"

Water frequently gets a back seat. Because it's so common for most of us in the United States, we don't realize how important it is. A lot of people like drinking anything other than water. As I received feedback from people who purchased these products from me, I discovered the number one thing they would say is: *I like water now!* Those words are music to my ears. I was so happy to hear that I was sharing a technology with people that was allowing them to experience water differently.

The feedback channels weren't limited to people. I also received great feedback from my garden. In my first year of gardening with structured water, I was still in a stage where I was doing my best to keep myself neutral and ask the universe to show me the proof. *If structured water was really so good, then it should be easy for me to detect.*

This proof came through when I had an outrageous crop in my garden. There was a farm down the street, and their corn stalks were approximately eight feet tall; my stalks were twelve feet tall. I couldn't even jump high enough to touch the tops of them. I was astounded. In addition, my produce was so abundant that my family couldn't keep up with eating all the produce, so we opened a farm stand. We put a little jar out and allowed people the joy of purchasing living foods from the edge of our yard.

That lesson amazed me and helped affirm my confidence in structured water. After all, my cells and plant cells are very similar. If it was happening in the garden, I knew it must be happening inside me too. I did not expect to grow twelve feet tall, but if I could come back into alignment with my divine blueprint, with the way my body was designed to be, that seemed like it would lead to a much better life.

The most interesting thing that happened in the garden happened in a different year. The day I went to plant my tomato plants in my structured water hydrated garden, it was very cold. I made a choice to dig holes deeper for my tomato plants, put the root ball down lower, and cover up part of the stem. As the summer progressed, my plants were doing poorly, and I wasn't sure why.

At the same time, I was learning about inflammation in my body, and coming to the conclusion that my body was suffering from it. I learned that one of the foods that contributes to inflammation is tomatoes. As my tomato plants were not producing extensively, a weed called purslane was multiplying prolifically. There was so much purslane on the ground in the garden that I could weed for hours on a single day, and then within just a few days later, it would be back again. This was happening over and over again.

Finally, I stopped to ask water. I stood in my garden and said, "I don't understand what's going on here. I'm not getting tomatoes, and I'm getting a ton of purslane. Why?"

I was guided to research purslane, and I discovered that purslane is a highly compacted source of omega oils. My garden was producing the omega oils that I needed, while not producing the tomatoes that would have caused more inflammation. As I saw the whole picture and realized how all of this was happening in water, I came to understand the power of structured water.

I don't know if I can find the words to explain the difference that it makes for me, living my daily life exposed to infinite energy. I used to think I was in charge of my life, and I needed to create the results. That life was filled with pressure and fear because I always felt like I wasn't doing a good enough job.

These experiences with structured water have helped me to see that the Law of Oneness is a universal law. Everything that happens is happening to help me remember how to be blissful. I believe it is our birthright and our nature to be blissful, and water is gently tapping us on the shoulder all the time, giving us experiences and insights that move us deeper and deeper in this direction.

> *Produce soaked or rinsed in structured water keeps literally weeks in my fridge, and since I buy mostly organics, I am relieved to see my grocery bill has shrunk noticeably. Another benefit is in taste: fairly bitter greens I eat daily, like kale, dandelion greens, mustard or collards, seem far sweeter!*

I water my organic veggie garden with structured water—the result is faster-growing, bigger, healthier plants, and no pests. My house plants cheer when they see me coming with the pitcher, and sunflower seeds I sprout for eating thrive and grow at an unprecedented pace.

~ Shira N.

CHAPTER THREE

The ABCs of Water Filtration

BIG QUESTIONS

If you're like me, you probably want the safest and best water for yourself and your family. With hydration involved in every process in our bodies, it's obviously important. However, it can be confusing to figure out which water treatment system is the best. There are so many different opinions, and as I found out, the situation is even more confusing than it looks like at the surface level.

Where Do You Get Your Information?

When I started this journey, I did research, consulting resources such as *Consumer Reports*, review websites, and water filtration company articles. The more I dug into those, the more I realized they all started from the same perspective. Everything was written to sell a product that has a replacement part. Everything was written to encourage the reader to become a lifelong customer of the company ultimately responsible for that style of thinking.

What people don't know, and what I didn't know back then, is that when you read that type of report, everything is about the world of chemistry and traditional water filtration. There's no mention or information about the physics of water—the energy of water. Given that everything is energy, this just doesn't make sense. When most people are receiving information, they don't even learn that structured water is a possibility.

I had the privilege in this business of becoming visible internationally. As a result, people called me from all over the world. No matter what country they were from or their accent, they always started the conversation with concerns about what should be removed from water, such as fluoride and chlorine. As I heard this same messaging coming from so many different voices, I realized people are encouraged to think this way by the system.

What Is Safe Water?

Let's start with what safe water isn't. Bottled water, whether in glass or plastic, is *not* safe water. It is not safe for our species to have a disposable or a convenience mindset, to think that there's some place called *over there*, and when we send out our trash or recyclables, things mysteriously go *away*. There is no away!

I learned as the chairman of the recycling committee that some recyclables, like plastic bottles, are shipped on barges to countries like India, then incinerated. When those toxins go into the air, that air is on the same Earth you're living on. So, you think that there's an *away*, but there really isn't.

If you buy a plastic water bottle, one-quarter of the ounces of that water—let's say you had a sixteen-ounce bottle, four ounces of that—would be filled with oil. That's how much energy it takes to produce, transport, and dispose of that plastic bottle. Glass bottles are also not safe because they directly contribute to trash gyres discussed earlier. Even though most of us recycle our glass bottles, many of these bottles are actually not recycled and find their way to our trash dumps.

It's also not safe financially. We spend $21 billion globally per year on water bottles. It's extraordinary. Bottled water is a marketing bonanza. It is amazing that marketers can convince so many people to purchase something that comes from another person's tap almost for free and then convince them to buy it for a dollar.

Water Filters Can Be Confusing

Bottled water is not a safe solution. As I explored water filters, I found that they don't meet the promises I expected from them either. When I was putting my reputation on the line by telling people that there was a best, traditional chemistry-based filter to use, I wanted to see the reports that showed the toxins being removed from the water.

So, I would contact companies and say: *Send me your lab reports.* They would ignore me, and because I was persistent, eventually they would answer. I heard things like: *Well, we use a material in our filters that was tested by the manufacturer of the material. We don't actually test our filters for contaminant removal because we take the word of the manufacturer.*

I was stunned! These are the companies promising us safe water, and some of them aren't even testing the actual products they're selling to us. When they do test it, they will often test one contaminant in isolation in the lab, and that's not the way contaminants work in your water or your home. They come en masse in your water, and a filter—if it were going to do a good job of making the water safe—would have to remove all those toxins together.

Finally, the promise of removal is actually a practice of reduction. Very, very few filters remove anything completely from water. Almost all of them leave anywhere from 1 percent to 50 percent of the contaminant they're supposed to be removing. Additionally, no water filters address the energetic signature of the toxins in the water.

What About the Energy of Water?

I love to look at things from a holistic perspective, and I enjoy testing theories with knowledge from other domains of life to see how they hold up. One of the perspectives I have explored is homeopathy. I know there are many thousands of practitioners around the world who use homeopathy with great results.

Homeopathic remedies are created by putting a physical substance into water or alcohol. Then two things are done to it. It is *succussed*—which means shaking it—and then diluted. It is succussed and diluted, succussed and diluted. If a substance is succussed and diluted once at a ratio of 1:10

or X, that remedy is designated with a potency of 1X. If it's done thirty times, it's 30X.

Homeopathic medicines are effective and used globally. Yet they are, from a chemical basis, simply water. Once a homeopathic medicine is diluted by twenty-six times—26X or more—the physical substance present at the beginning is gone. I applied that concept to water filtration and particularly to the idea of reduction rather than removal. I saw that, no matter what toxin somebody was trying to remove from water with one of the filters, the energetic residue of that toxin was still in the water. So, homeopathy provided me with a great insight into the possibility of an energetic process to make safe water.

I tried to explain this to my mom. Like a lot of people, she was really confused.

"What do you mean by structured water?" she'd ask. "What does that mean? Isn't it water? It's water! What are you talking about, structuring the water and energy?"

Imagine a single hydrogen atom. Imagine it expanding to the size of a football field. In that scale, the nucleus is the size of a tennis ball, and the electrons are orbiting somewhere around the perimeter of the stadium. Between the nucleus and electrons, there is all that empty space. However, do not think there's nothing in that space. Everything is permeated by energy, so there are enormous potential and space for even a single hydrogen atom to be taking on different forms of energy.

I don't know if that explanation is going to work for everyone. People need to move out of the mindset that objects are super-solid—nothing can fit in between atoms—and realize there's actually a lot of empty space in whatever appears solid. Then, they can understand that there's something there, and everything is energy.

CREATING A SYSTEM

As I pierced through the illusions of the available information, I recognized I was delving into a deeper level of research than most people would probably do for themselves. It made sense because I was doing it full time, but I felt the need to take everything I was learning and condense it into a system that would allow people to be clear about their own circumstances and to find a water treatment system that meets their needs.

Self-Empowerment

Based on my observations, I've noticed that most systems encourage ordinary people like you and me to defer our power to an expert. The education system and the media system strongly influence us to think this way. They say only those who have certain scientific criteria have the right to define a situation and the principles involved.

This has never felt right to me. It conflicts with the spiritual teaching that all the answers to all the problems I have lie within. As I've responded to the call for safe water systems and for a solution to the plastic bottle industry, I've wanted to ensure that I offered a system that is about personal empowerment.

I want you to feel empowered to make choices in your life from your own knowing and from what resonates with you. I want to shift the conversation from the typical language of reverse osmosis, carbon filter, charcoal filter, sink filter, and whole house, to one where you can look at the water you are dealing with and make a choice based on your circumstances.

Before I share the system with you, I want to share a closing word about your personal empowerment regarding saving money and water testing. I've never felt the need to have a water test done. That's because I look at the Earth as one big, connected pool of water. There's a water company a few miles down the road from me that is sending water from reservoirs and local water-gathering places out through pipes to my home.

The water that I'm using goes through the pipes and maybe picks up a little bit of the material in the pipes while doing that. Truthfully, that's just a minor contribution to the total content of the water. I've found it simpler to look at the water quality report from my local municipality as a way of judging what's in my water and what I might be concerned about. If you would like to find information about your water without paying for it, just look up a water quality report for your town. I'm sure you'll find one online.

The Chemistry of Water

Now we're going to discuss the core of the issue. All traditional water filters are addressing the chemistry of water. They're looking at what's physically present in the water, and they're operating under the principles of removal or reduction—as we've already learned. To help you understand that, I've created a simple system that I call the ABCs of water filtration. I'm going to review four letters for you now: A, B, C, and D.

A is for *aesthetics*. Aesthetics refers to what you smell and taste. These are important components of water filtration. If people don't enjoy the taste of their water, they will very likely choose something else. An A-filter is one that removes things that smell or particles that don't taste good from the water. If a chemistry-based filter is not a quality A-filter, it will not last in the market. If a filter doesn't create good-tasting water and good-smelling water, people are not going to use it.

B is for *biologics*. Biologics deals with the viruses and pathogens that live in water. Prior to chlorinating water in 1907, our average life span was in the range of approximately forty-eight years. If we fast-forward to fifty years after we started chlorinating water, we were expected to live for sixty years. This was a massive shift. We were killing the water-borne viruses and pathogens that were so harmful to people's lives.

If you live in a part of the world that has chlorination or other methods—like UV— of killing biological materials, you don't need a B-filter. You only need this if you're concerned about living viruses and bacteria in water.

C is for *chemicals*. We live in a world that relies heavily on commercial agriculture and industry. There are over 80,000 different toxins in our environment now, and over 2,000 new ones every year.[3] All these toxins are considered chemicals, and a C-filter is one that removes chemicals.

D is for *dissolved solids*. This is a category focused on what happens in the pipes on the way to your faucet. If you have really old pipes, you may want a D-filter. This filter removes lead or copper. It is designed to remove heavy metals that are leaching into your water.

That's the A, B, C, and D of water filtration.

---

3 Scialla, Mark. "It could take centuries for EPA to test all the unregulated chemicals under a new landmark bill." PBS New Hour. pbs.org/newshour/science/it-could-take-centuries-for-epa-to-test-all-the-unregulated-chemicals-under-a-new-landmark-bill

The Physics of Water

E is for *energy*. This letter took me years to figure out. I was so well versed in A, B, C, and D because I tried tons and tons of different filters and engaged with lots of people. I found out I was only dealing with chemistry; I wasn't giving people a real difference maker in their lives. I was giving them an improvement but not making a difference.

When I got to E, everything changed. I learned that there's something in water called *hydrogen bond angles,* and the way hydrogen and oxygen are bonded together can change. I learned that toxins can be neutralized energetically. This statement doesn't make sense to a linear mind that's been trained in chemistry.

In fact, one of the most interesting aspects of my occupation is when someone calls me after they've heard me interviewed or seen an article I've written. They try to ask me questions about the *energy* of water, but their whole vocabulary has been conditioned in the *chemistry* of water. They don't know how to ask questions in this new language, the language based on transforming what's in water. It's based on letting water clean itself.

We live in a vibrational universe. I don't know about you, but I'm still coming to understand what this means. As we unfold that reality and understand that everything is energy, we're going to find new solutions to old problems. We're going to approach things from a new level of consciousness.

The field is the sole governing agency of the particle.
~ Albert Einstein

Now that you know the ABCs of water filtration, you can consider your own personal concerns. We'll discuss this later in more depth, but I want to ask you one empowering question now.

Is your thinking about your water oriented toward understanding the A, B, C, D, or does the E intrigue you and empower you to learn more?

When you implement solutions for yourself, you may want to consider choosing the E strategy first. If you choose this physics of water as your water treatment system and release the old paradigm of the chemistry of water, the physics-based devices typically come with a one-time purchase, no replacement parts, and no maintenance. You will be freeing yourself to a lifetime of great water with a one-time purchase, and I think that's an important consideration.

STRUCTURED WATER SCIENCE

With the dawning of the age of Aquarius, we are experiencing enormous shifts in our understanding about water. Countless academics and scientists around the world are sharing new discoveries. These discoveries are frequently referred to by different names: *structured water, activated water, hexagonal water, fourth phase water,* H_3O_2, and *exclusion zone water.* No matter what you call it, they all point to the same thing. There is a type of water we haven't understood previously, and it's very different.

Fourth Phase of Water

In 2013, Gerald Pollack, the head of the University of Washington's bioengineering department, published a book titled, *The Fourth Phase of Water* (Ebner and Sons Publishers, 2013). In it, he provides scientific proof for this new science of water that's being studied and spoken about in so many laboratories around the world. I chose to profile his work because his book is easily accessible—you can get a copy yourself if you'd like to go deeper into the science—and he touches on some important points that help us understand this new phase of water.

A lot of people think they know what percentage of our body is made of water. Typically, they answer 70 or 80 percent. Well, that's not exactly true. We're born at about 95 percent water, and then, as we age, the percentage declines and can go to as low as 50 percent. Seventy or 80 percent is a good average, but it's not necessarily accurate for the majority of people.

What Dr. Pollack published is that by count, by number, 99 percent of the molecules in our bodies are water molecules. Virtually *everything* is a water molecule because they're so teeny-tiny.

Why is this important?

Whatever force created this universe, and your body and mine, it deemed the most important substance—the thing that is in everything—to be water.

Dr. Pollack also shares with us that water is not just H_2O. People typically think of it as two hydrogen atoms bonded to an oxygen atom, when in fact, there are billions of interactions happening every second. The hydrogen bond angles in water can shift. As these shifts were happening, he detected H_3O_2 and OH-, and many other configurations of the chemistry of water.

The most important concept from Dr. Pollack is this new phase of water—which he calls *fourth-phase* or *exclusion zone* water—acts like a battery. You can insert energy into the battery, and then that energy can come out in people, plants, animals, in everything. If you want to have an energized self, one of the best ways to accomplish this is to fill ourselves with energized water.

Live Blood Cell Analysis

As a financial advisor, I experienced firsthand the implosion in our economy that occurred when derivatives blew up in 2008. When we got down to the heart of those derivatives, we found out they didn't work in the real world. They worked in theory: they impressed academics and scientists, and seemed like good tools, but when we asked, "How do they impact people's lives?" the impact was devastating.

Through this experience, I learned the value of listening to client feedback as a source of collective wisdom and have always wanted to know: *Yeah, but what difference does it make in people's lives?*

I had an opportunity to do some testing with a nutritionist who does live blood cell analysis. We met at a conference in Las Vegas, and when people arrived, we asked them if they had ever experienced structured water. Those who said no we invited to be part of our test group. We took them upstairs and immediately measured their blood under a microscope, showing them what their blood looked like.

We then asked them to participate in the conference as they would have before, and to not do anything differently. They didn't know we had equipped the conference with structured water. All the water they were drinking was now fourth-phase, exclusion zone, or structured water.

Forty-eight hours later, we drew blood samples again and the results were amazing.

The nutritionist said to me, "Patrick, I've been looking at people's blood for 11 years, and I have prescribed nutritional therapies to address their deficiencies. In forty-eight hours, I saw greater changes in *every* participant than I've seen with the best thirty days of nutritional therapy for anybody. I am so blown away by how effective structured water is!"

When I saw those results, I knew we were onto something and many of those who went through live analysis sought me out to buy structured water devices. I knew we were moving in the right direction when people were actively demonstrating the difference that structured water makes in their lives.

The Best Proof of All

I feel so grateful to be living the career that I'm living now. I especially appreciate that I'm able to reach people all over the globe and impact their lives through sharing the benefits of structured water.

One of the things I love most about my career is the great variety of responses I receive from people all over the world about how structured water impacts their lives. So many experience significant improvements in their personal health and wellness, and that of their families. In addition, people feel a closer connection with their environment, knowing that their choice of structured water benefits all on a local and global level.

However, there's been a surprising impact upon the spiritual aspects of life for many as well. I personally had no idea when I started with structured water that it was going to expand my creativity, sense of connection, and even my spirituality.

I've come to understand that structured water is *the* substance that connects everything.

Here are some of the impacts my clients have experienced:

- Increased enjoyment of and desire for water
- Renewed sense of health and vitality
- Healthier, more vibrant-feeling skin
- Decreased joint and muscle pain
- Stronger, more radiant-looking hair
- Increased sense of joy and happiness
- Improved quality of sleep
- Balanced emotional state
- Decreased headaches
- Improved digestion
- Loss of excess weight
- Increased vibration

Structured water is the operating system made for the human body. It's what we were made to run on, and immersing one's life in structured water is a pathway to love and joy. Take a look below and see the variety of extraordinary experiences our customers have shared with us.

> *The water tastes very smooth. It's almost like I'm drinking velvet water. What an amazing experience!*
> ~ Jacqueline L.

> *I was looking to regain my energy and strength following breast cancer treatment, which left me*

lethargic. I feel like I have my life back. I have energy and even went to the gym for Spin Class twice this week! Woo-hoo!

~ Dana E.

Thank you, Patrick! It came yesterday and I am so far impressed with the changes I am seeing. Increased energy on all four levels—physical, emotional, mental, and spiritual! I love the sweet taste! Last time water tasted like that was from a clear mountain stream high in the mountains far away from people! I am warmer. I think that means my circulation is better. It may also mean that my thyroid is working better. I am experiencing better balance on my right and left sides of my body. I slept better. I had happy dreams that I could remember, which is a first in many years. I woke up happy and feeling good. It has been years since I could say that.

I noticed all of this in the first twenty-four hours. I am looking forward to more changes that I can't even imagine right now!

Thank you very much! Have a wonderful day!

~ Lyn

CHAPTER FOUR

Living Water Transforms Hydration and Your Flow With Life

HYDRATION AND FLOW

It's so easy to get caught up in how others think about hydration but this doesn't reflect what's truly possible for us. Most talk about hydration in terms of the number of glasses of water they consume in a day, and never even consider whether that water is truly alive.

Does the water you drink have energy and vitality like in nature, or has it lost its living essence due to traveling through long, straight pipes or been stored in plastic bottles?

When I fill my body with living water, I experience not only the physical benefits of hydration but also the spiritual benefits of being in the flow with life.

We're Not Doing It Right

Many studies involving hundreds and even thousands of people conclude that over 90% of us are chronically dehydrated. Renowned triple-board certified Zach Bush, MD, an expert in modern dis-ease epidemics and innovative projects for promoting human health and longevity, goes further, and states that 100% of us are dehydrated at some point in our days.[4] I have been putting this to an informal real-world test over the last many years. By observing the number of people with dry lips, brain fog, and low energy, I would have to agree with Zach Bush.

So here is the most important process in our bodies, and almost nobody is doing it right. There's a significant impact on our lives for this mistake, but we're not used to connecting that impact to hydration. I think a lot of us overlook the potential benefits that are sitting within easy reach.

This brings to mind a beautiful example of how the benefits of hydration with structured water supports emotional health as well as harmony within our relationships.

When my daughter, Amanda, first started attending middle school, I would pick her up after school on Thursdays. My three other children would already be in the car and as we joked around, it would create a fun and playful environment.

---

4 For interviews with Dr. Zach Bush, MD, visit hydrationfoundation.org.

However, when Amanda would join us, I would notice a significant shift to that of heavier, more agitated energy. During the first three Thursdays of that school year, this shift would become so apparent that I became terrified of her "attitude" for it seemed to trigger an intense annoyance of my mere presence within her.

Finally, after the third Thursday, I thought to ask how much water she drank throughout the day. She replied, "None, Dad. It's not cool to drink water in middle school."

I was astounded and promptly apologized to her. I was certainly not living up to my life's mission if I wasn't able to recognize, let alone shift perspectives to that of drinking water being healthy and "cool," even in middle school.

I vowed to transform this cultural perspective and we developed a new system within our family. Going forward, each day I picked her up from school, I handed her a bottle of structured water and she agreed to drink it before engaging with any of us. If she wasn't willing to do this, she could take the bus home, which took significantly longer and was a much less comfortable ride.

As Amanda started rehydrating with structured water, her entire energy and emotions shifted. As a family, we learned that when any of us are moody or are not feeling well, we share a bottle of structured water and it helps that person transition into a better state of being.

Interestingly, this practice is backed by a study conducted by the University of Connecticut which found that even mild dehydration (at a 1.36 percent dehydration level) is sufficient enough to cause decreases in mood and cognitive abilities.[5] We knew this from personal experience and have now made it a habit of tending to our emotions with water.

Another story I'd like to share comes from Dr. Alexis Carrel (1873–1944). He was a Nobel Prize winner and physiologist:

> *The cell is immortal. It is merely the fluid in which it floats that degenerates. Renew this fluid at regular intervals, give the cells what they require for nutrition, and as far as we know, the pulsation of life can go on forever.*

He conducted experiments over thirty years and determined if he changed the fluid surrounding chicken heart cells, they lived four times longer than usual simply by having their waste removed on a daily basis. Based on this work, we can see that detoxification is one of the great opportunities that comes with hydration and flow with life.

Just Water

I really love and honor water, so I notice the way people talk about it. I notice if you go to a restaurant and somebody orders water, they'll often say: *I'll have just water, please,*

---

5 Armstrong, L. E., et al. "Mild dehydration affects mood in healthy young women." PubMed. February, 2012. DOI: 10.3945/jn.111.142000

as though they need an excuse for choosing the elixir the Creator of the Universe designed as the optimal fuel for the human body.

It's so funny that people scurry about their busy lives, always wanting more and thinking they need to gain advantages for themselves and their family, when they have such an underutilized resource—optimal energy for the human body—potentially sitting right in their hand. They completely overlook the glass of water. Perhaps because water is so ubiquitous, people have determined that it's not very important, but I believe it's the most important substance in life.

Consider this example of scientific evidence. Information traveling from the sun that would take minutes to travel here— say, an explosion on the surface of the sun—is transferred instantaneously and measurably in water molecules, minutes before that information could travel from the sun to the Earth. There's a connectivity between water molecules; they're all sharing information at the same time.

Water is not *just water* to me; it's nature's elixir.

Intracellular / Extracellular Hydration and the Aquaporin Channel

The science of hydration has been deepening over the last few years. In 2003, there was a Nobel Prize awarded for the discovery of the *aquaporin channel,* to Dr. Peter Agre from Johns Hopkins University. His discovery showed there is a way for water to flow into cells quickly and efficiently, and there are also situations where water cannot penetrate the cells.[6] This has helped me understand the concept of intracellular and extracellular hydration.

There are two types of hydration:

1. Extracellular hydration consists of water that passes through the body quickly. It's as if you don't receive any benefit from it. For example, if you've ever consumed a beverage—a coffee, a tea, a sports drink, etc. —and noticed not long after drinking it that you needed to pee a lot; it's as though the beverage went right through your body. It didn't sink in. It didn't go into the intracellular cavities.

2. Intracellular hydration consists of water that can electrically interface with cells and is necessary for real hydration. You have probably been misled that any water will increase hydration at the cellular level because *water is water because it is wet*. However, water has to contain energy in order to function effectively, let alone efficiently, at the cellular level.

With all the money to be made marketing beverages, bottled water, juices with sugar, caffeine, and food, companies have

---

6 Agre, Peter. "The Aquaporin Water Channels." America Thoracic Society. March, 2006. DOI: 10.1513/pats.200510-109JH

convinced people that the best energy sources for their body are the ones that can be used to make corporate profits. We need to recognize by putting living water into our bodies in a way that consistently moves into the cells, into those intracellular cavities, we're going to be giving ourselves the energy source that our bodies were really created to run on.

ELEMENTS OF HYDRATION

Did you know that a prune is just a dehydrated plum?

It's true! The only difference between the two is water content. When I look at older people, I see kind of the same situation. I see a lot of people in their seventies, eighties, and nineties who look more like prunes than plums. I don't want to have a body where my shoulders turn inward, my height shrinks a little bit, or my skin wrinkles. So, I'm running an experiment with my life. Maybe, just maybe, the most important thing in life is hydration. If I can keep as much water as possible in my intracellular cavities, maybe I can become more plum-like as I go through life. I don't want to be dehydrated. I don't want to lose the flow and experience the resistance that comes with that loss.

The Hydration Dashboard

The first step you need to take to be successful with hydration and to flow with life is knowing your own status report.

What is your dashboard for hydration?

How do you know if your hydration processes is effective?

The obvious place that most people look is their urine color and sometimes its scent. In general, the darker the color of urine, the more dehydrated a person is, and it's a good idea to drink enough so your urine is clear to slightly yellow.

One area I've noticed is *the way my skin feels*. Imagine the way your skin feels in the wintertime—particularly if you live in a drier, less humid, colder environment. You have probably experienced your skin drier in the winter, then softer in the summer. Start noticing your skin daily rather than on a seasonal basis. Notice that when you're taking care of yourself through hydration, your skin feels moist. That's a great way to discover hydration.

There's also another easy area to be aware of, which is *the inside of your cheeks*. I noticed this while drinking reverse osmosis water and while drinking tea. Both of those are actually dehydrating beverages for me. They leave the inside of my mouth feeling dry. Now that I've tuned in to this, I think it's an earlier warning mechanism than thirst, and I'm able to put water into my body more often, just by noticing that my cheeks are feeling dry. I don't have to wait until I am dehydrated enough to experience a loss in cognitive function or shift in emotions.

Other areas for you to look at are your *energy levels,* your *creativity,* and your *emotions.* Since I made living water my vocation, I have had a surge in energy, creativity, and emotional stability. I experience love and joy as my overriding emotions much more frequently and fluidly. When I think about a new topic, I can access infinite levels of creativity much more easily. If you find yourself stuck or feeling lower-vibration emotions, start playing with hydration and see if adding more water to your body helps you in this way.

Best Practices

Here are three practices I recommend exploring:

1. The quality of the water that you drink
2. The container or the process that you drink it from
3. The frequency and habits you have

After years of experimenting, I've determined that altering the physics of water, the energy of the water, is the most important consideration for me. Probably 99 percent of the water I consume now has either been put into a structured water device or passed through one before consuming it. My experiences have shown me I feel better if I have water that is treated using principles of physics.

Regardless of whether you align with my preference, you must *drink water that you love* to be hydrated and flowing with life. That's step one.

The next step is to *have a container that you love to drink from* and a process that you enjoy. For me, I like drinking out of glass. It's crisp and clean-tasting water, and I don't have the perception of leaching plastics or dirt picked up in any way. Choose a container or water bottle that you love.

Next, make sure you practice good habits. One of the most empowering tips I can share is: Always know where your next fill-up is coming from. I'll give you an example. When I go to bed at night, I take a bottle of water, put it in a VitaJuwel gemstone water bottle, and place it next to my bedside table.

This serves two purposes. I usually sleep through the night and once I wake up in the morning, my first bottle of water is immediately available. I do my best to drink this quickly because I know that after seven, eight, or nine hours of sleep, I'm usually dehydrated. Additionally, if I do wake in the middle of the night and desire water, it's right there next to me.

Everybody is dehydrated when they wake up in the morning. I like to put at least the first seventeen ounces in quickly. Then, as soon as I finish my first water bottle, I fill it again. So, I have my second one full, but I just drank a bunch of water. That's the way I keep going throughout the day. Whenever I'm drinking down the bottle that I have, I'm mindful of when and where I'm going to fill it up again.

Sometimes when I leave home, I need to fill a one-gallon glass container and take it with me in the car so that when my seventeen-ounce container is emptied, I can refill it with high-quality, living water. Always *know where your next fill-up is coming from,* and drink steadily and consistently. Drinking before you feel thirsty is the best practice I know to help you stay hydrated.

The Low-Hanging Fruit

Recently, I did a twenty-eight-day fruit cleanse. All I ate was fruit, and I ate a lot of melons during that month. What surprised me was that when I was eating the melons, I didn't want as much water as I normally do. That's how I discovered for myself the proof of what people say about living foods, like fruits and vegetables, having high water content. That's actually a hydrating aspect of lifestyle.

As you are developing hydration habits in your body, you might want to pay attention to fruits and vegetables that have the highest water content.

As an aside, I want to share that if you've been dehydrated your whole life, it can take a little while to rehydrate your body. I want to encourage you to have patience and to practice self-compassion.

When I was first experimenting with better water habits, I drank alkaline water for more than a year. During that time, I had a daily goal and had to force myself to drink that amount every day. Looking back, it felt like work and it took a year and a half for my cells to become adequately hydrated.

Luckily, I've learned a lot since then and in transitioning to drinking structured water, I have experienced firsthand a shift in rehydration to be much faster and more effective than ever before. Within days, I began experiencing increased energy levels, steadier moods, and clearer thinking, and within weeks I enjoyed more refreshing sleep, a greater sense of peace, connection to my creativity, and softer skin. You now have an opportunity to experience these tremendous benefits of rehydration for yourself.

Did you know there's a hydrating benefit to movement?

Gina Bria from the Hydration Foundation is an anthropologist who is bringing to light information about the role of fascia and movement in hydration. One of the things that she talks about is how people who live in the desert stay hydrated. Clearly, they are not drinking those eight glasses a day that so many people are conditioned to think is important. Gina has co-authored a book with Dr. Dana Cohen, MD called *Quench: Beat Fatigue, Drop Weight, and Heal Your Body* (2018), that teaches us that real hydration is achieved by what you drink and eat and how you move.

There must be other sources of hydration, and movement is an important place to look. Notice what impact it has on your own body when you move. While I'm writing this book, I am doing simple micro-movements at my desk.

Simple micro-movements you can do:

- Move your chin up and down
- Move your neck
- Roll your neck from side to side
- Roll your ankles around
- Lift your legs off the floor

See what benefits you experience from keeping your body moving. It may be as simple as that movement is increasing your hydration, and that's part of why it feels good.

TRANSFORMATIONAL NINJAS: HOW TO GET UNSTUCK FROM THE MUCK

Now we're coming to my favorite part of this book. I had no idea when I started going down the rabbit hole that I was going to learn that water is related to the significant challenges I see humanity now facing. They are directly connected. I see the pathway as not only hydrating our physical bodies, but also moving into the flow with our spiritual bodies. This access to our spiritual side will change so many things in life.

We've been trained to focus on sugar, caffeine, and food for energy, but we want to sparkle and shine. That shine comes from a higher level of consciousness, which is available when we immerse our lives in living water.

The gateway to a life beyond your wildest dreams begins with understanding this concept: *multi-dimensional living is accomplished through immersion in living water.*

Turning Lead Into Gold (Alchemy)

I've always been fond of alchemy and the idea of turning lead into gold. Recently, I realized this process is not about a physical truth, where we actually take a pile of lead, turn it into gold, and then all of a sudden, we're miraculously rich. It's actually a story about us. It's a story about taking our lives from gray, ashen, and lead-like and making them shimmering and shining like the sun, or like gold. The way we do that is by creating a state I describe as *radiance* in our lives.

We achieve radiance on the physical level in our live blood cells. Remember the testing where people's blood changed in just forty-eight hours? There's another measurement of this, taken with *gas discharge visualization* (GDV). GDV, created by a Russian scientist, is used all over the world as a measurement tool for the energy of organic substances, such as water, and even whole organisms, such as our bodies. Scientists using GDV have discovered that when people drink living water for the first time, they experience an expansion in their energy field—a minimum increase of 10 percent. This is the physical shimmering and shining I reference when I speak of performing alchemy in our own lives.

Opening the Third Eye

The first country to use fluoride in a public water system was Germany, just before the start of World War II. Many people claim this was done to help keep the population docile and open to propaganda or mind control.

Since then, there's a lot more information substantiating that fluoride, when introduced into our bodies, calcifies our pineal gland, which is part of our pituitary gland.[7]

Fluoridation causes a dampening of our connection to the unified field, the field that connects all there is. So, when people call me for a safe water solution, they often want to remove fluoride from the water. I tell them a few stories.

First, while drinking structured water, I've experienced the opening of my third eye. The first time I felt that, I was driving down the highway. I received an intuition to get off at the next exit. My kids were with me, and we were late for the rehearsal dinner for my little brother's wedding. They couldn't understand why I was getting off the highway. I said, "Just get your phones out, and figure out how we're going to change roads here."

We did, and as we started on a new path on back roads, they told me if we had continued past the exit, we would

---

7 Mercola, Joseph. "The Healthy Drink that May Destroy Your Sleep." Mercola. 09 August 2011. articles.mercola.com/sites/articles/archive/2011/08/09/fluoride-and-pineal-gland.aspx

have been in a four-mile backup. I had no way of knowing that with my conscious mind, but I had an intuitive sense that showed me the need to take an action. Since I began experimenting, I've come to understand this is my third eye, another sense we human beings have. When we decalcify our pineal gland, we gain access to it.

I now have the wisdom to make choices in my life, to flow with life, and to hear more about where life is guiding me, rather than doing things from my mind.

Additionally, I now know when my third eye is open or closed, which brings me to a second story: I went on vacation with my family—my mother, stepdad, and brothers I grew up with. While I was with them, I ate meat, I ate pies, and I didn't focus on my structured water. When I came home, I returned to my home office where I spend a lot of time. I'm used to being creative in this space. I came in and I couldn't feel my third eye.

I'm accustomed to feeling it all the time, and if it's not palpable, I can take one breath or one sip of water to reactivate it. When I came back from seven days with my family, I was a little distraught that I couldn't feel it. I went for walks down at the beach. I played music patterned with sacred geometry. I took showers. I drank lots of water. It took more than a day for my third eye to reopen. That's when I realized how much I value living in this open state and having a palpable, minute-by-minute connection with my third eye.

Finally, a third story is from a customer. She told me she has thrown up every time she drank fluoridated water throughout her life. She has a strong reaction to it. When she drank water through one of our devices, she didn't throw up. She sampled it at her naturopathic doctor's office, and she wanted to buy a device because she couldn't believe our device could transform fluoride and make it not harmful.

Coherence

Have you ever gone snorkeling and seen a school of fish swimming together, the way they seem to share a higher native intelligence, the way they turn at the same time to move in a new direction?

Maybe you've looked toward the sky and witnessed a group of geese joyfully honking their way in V-formation across the sky. In that V-formation, the front goose is breaking the wind for the ones behind it, making it easier for the flock, and the species, to move forward.

In contrast, when I turn on the television or absorb any media, I see a species that's at war with itself: human beings.

When I changed my personal identification within life from mind-based to heart-based — activating my pineal gland at the same time — I changed the way I think about and relate to everything. The rule of oneness became the rule of my life. I now see that everything, *everything*, that happens in life is supporting me to live a life of love, joy, and bliss.

It is my dream that as you find living water for yourself, you may open your superpowers and remember how to be a transformational ninja. You'll remember your role in helping not only yourself but others within humanity and the environment to become unstuck from the muck.

We have an incredible opportunity to embrace and transcend significant global obstacles right now, and my role is to help people understand:

1. Water is a living energy.

2. When we immerse our lives in that energy, it changes us.

3. When we change, we create a different world for everyone.

What is your role?

Humanity is counting on you. It's time we find this out together.

> *People have noticed a difference in me and asked me what I am doing. I tell them I am drinking structured water. My eighteen-year-old son calls it God Water. He was completely joking when he first said this, but what he later told me what he meant is that it is amazing and God would want us to drink amazing water. Pretty smart for an eighteen-year-old boy, I think.*
>
> ~ Regards, Holly

CHAPTER FIVE

Choosing the Best Water for You and Your Family

ANALOGY

When I was a financial advisor, I learned I could come up with the data to make any point that I wanted to and make a justifiable argument to present it. I despised that there wasn't truth; there was simply the person holding the data and what they wanted to prove with it.

My experience is that most science is bought and paid for these days by an agenda. The agenda usually has an economic benefit to the person or company pushing the data, and I despise that too. For this book to matter, for my vocation to matter, for my inquiry into water to matter, it must make a difference in *your* life. If it doesn't inspire *you* to take new action in your life, or make a difference in your ability to be self-empowered and make choices, then I'm not interested in delivering it.

We have a world right now with 94 percent of people dehydrated—at least—and we have trash gyres floating in our oceans. We have significant problems and yet have a tremendous opportunity to embrace concepts that can shift and transform our consciousness, and the world along with it.

People see water as ordinary, rather than seeing water as a multi-dimensional consciousness, carrying messages of oneness.

The concepts I share in this book have helped me to develop that perspective, and it's my intention to share them with you so you feel empowered to make the best decisions for yourself, your family, and the world around you. All issues pertaining to water are local in nature, so if after reading this, you don't feel like you have all the answers you need, then please visit TheWellnessEnterprise.com, and we'll help you dive deeper into how you can transform your health, life and world through structured water.

In my journey, there hasn't been a blueprint for me to follow. I don't feel like anybody else has done this in the way I have. I've turned to the universe for help, many times throwing my hands up in the air, literally, and said, "Okay, I don't understand! What do I do now?"

When I wanted to understand the difference between chemistry-based filters and physics-based structuring devices, the universe offered an analogy, an analogy based on transportation.

Most people use self-propelled transportation. They're drinking water that is treated with a filter, comes in a plastic bottle, or goes through long, straight pipes and comes out of a tap. None of those processes revitalize the water from an energetic standpoint, so when this water goes into your body, your cells need to work to convert that water to be useful and enter into intracellular cavities.

That's like being on a skateboard; you must use your own energy to move yourself forward. People are wasting a lot of potential energy by converting their water when it can easily be done for them.

If the traditional ways of treating water are like a filter or a bicycle, the physics-based devices are like a modern automobile. Imagine riding around on a bicycle your whole life, and then you try a car where you get in, turn a key, and go seventy miles an hour. That's outrageous!

Imagine how your body would feel when it experiences that level of energy and freedom inside. Let's look at this chapter through this lens of the transportation analogy.

Water Filters

First, let's consider what's in your mind already.

Having spoken to thousands of people around the world, I know most people think about filters and removing things from water. One of the decisions that you need to make to feel confident about your water choice for you and your family is to choose whether to filter or not.

Let me say this: Water filters are optional. There are many factors to evaluate in these decisions we're going to consider. What I'm asking you to do, since I know you're thinking about filters already, is to hold that point for a minute. Even though it's perhaps the one point you consider to me most important, let's make that decision last.

This decision will impact your:

- Health
- Finances
- Spirituality
- World around you

The best way to make an informed decision is to make sure you understand all these issues.

Water filters are great for reducing the concentration of toxins. Whether they create safe water is up to you to decide. In my experience, they're not good for the energetics of water.

They're not doing anything to remove the energy signatures of the toxins.

They're also not necessarily great for your wallet. A lot of businesses that exist in the world do not create a solution for the customer, but rather create a perpetual revenue stream for the business. Water filters are a perfect example.

If you find a tool that helps you filter water for twenty dollars every couple months, you might think that's an inexpensive solution. A lot of people think that way. If you need a new twenty-dollar solution every three months, four times a year to replace it, that is eighty dollars. Then, if you think about ten years, that's eight-hundred dollars. Remember, you were thinking: *I'm only spending twenty bucks.* When you consider filters, you need to figure the cost over time. You also need to think not just in terms of simple finances, but also in terms of the impact on your health, your vitality, your creativity, and your spirituality because those are all important costs to consider too.

Given what I've just shared with you about traditional filters being like self-propelled transportation, why would anybody want one?

There are two reasons: The first is because somebody has been conditioned to fear the toxins in their water, and they identify with those beliefs and want to act on them. That's fine. I'm not offering any judgment whether that's right or wrong. I'm letting you know that filters don't help with the energy of water. So, the first reason to want a filter is because you think you need it.

The second reason to use a filter is for taste. There are certain circumstances where the taste of water is just not as good through a structuring device as it is through a chemistry-based filter. For example, in parts of Florida the drinking water contains a significant amount of sulfur and in Las Vegas, it has very little interaction with nature and the earth.

If you find that the taste characteristics of your water, no matter what they are, are unpalatable to you, you might use a filter. In this case, choosing a simple, inexpensive one—in the ABCs of water filtration, we call this an A-based water filter—that changes the taste and odor of the water is understandable.

Structured Water Devices

Let's recap. I spent years learning to understand traditional water filters—in other words, changing the chemistry of water. I developed the ABCs of water filtration to A, B, C, and D, and I used this method to categorize chemistry-based water filters. When I started working with the physics of water, realizing that E is for energy, I realized that the physics-based devices might do some or of all the things that the chemistry-based devices do, so I explored a little bit further.

When I learned there are multiple physics-based devices on the market, I realized I needed some help. I literally asked water to tell me how to understand for myself the difference in chemistry-based filters and physics-based devices, and then how to discern among all the physics-based devices.

Chemistry, Physics, or Both

Now that you know about water filters and structured water devices, you face one obvious question:

Do I need both, or can I get by with one or the other?

I recommend that you start with structured water devices. The promises that go with structured water technology of increased energy, better cellular hydration, and a one-time purchase for the device without any repairs or maintenance make this the place to start. If you're satisfied with the structured water device without using a filter, you can make a one-time purchase and use it for the rest of your life.

Considering the question: *If I am going to buy a structured water device, can I get that first and experiment with it for thirty or sixty days, and then make a choice later about whether I need a filter?*

If you experience structured water for a month and aren't as excited about it as most of our customers are, then you can add a filter. If after reading this information, it just feels wrong not to reduce or remove toxins from your water, add a filter. If it doesn't feel right to choose transformation as your water purification system, and you really need the reduction or the removal to feel better, then buy it and recognize that your choices can change.

One of the problems people experience is they feel like when they make a water purification decision, it must be the one and only decision for their whole life. This choice can be a moving target, and it can change.

I've lived in the same house for nine years. In the first couple years I used filters, then I switched to structured water devices and stopped using filters. For about the last five years, I've only used structured water devices, except when one thing happened. About a year ago, my kitchen faucet was dripping consistently, and I needed to replace it.

When I replaced it, my water started tasting horrible, which didn't make any sense to me because I knew my water was structured. It tasted so bad that I ended up installing a filter and waited. What I discovered was faucets—like carpets, couches, and beds—off-gas. It took a couple of months of water running through my filter for that off-gassing process to be completed.

Even though I knew I was safe without a filter, I chose to use a filter for a couple of months and was glad that I did. So, you might find you want to go with a structuring device at one place—if you go somewhere on vacation and feel great about it—and other places you'll want to use a filter too.

How do you know which system to get?

The point of this book is to empower you so you can rely on yourself, rather than a so-called expert. I want to give you one of my best testing mechanisms: three days on, three days off. When I was testing a lot of different technologies, I discovered if I tried a certain behavior for three days, stopped it for three days, and repeated that process until clarity emerged, clarity usually emerged quickly. If you use the measuring tools, noticing whether the inside of your mouth feels wet, how your skin feels, your energy levels, and your sleep pattern, I think you can use those variables to determine in three days if something is serving you or not.

If you want to physically remove toxins from water, then buy a chemistry-based water filter. If you want to energetically neutralize and transform everything in water, purchase a physics-based structuring device. If you want it all, try both. They work together harmoniously, so you don't have to worry which one goes before the other or is going to degrade the other. One is taking care of chemistry; the other is taking care of physics. It's fine if you want both.

PUTTING YOUR ABCS INTO PRACTICE

Remember what I wrote in the beginning of the book, "For this book to matter, it has to make a difference in your life. If it doesn't inspire you to take new action, then it doesn't really matter." Let's review the ABCs of water filtration, designed to empower you to look at your personal water circumstances and make the best choice for safety and confidence for your family.

Aesthetics

The A in the ABCs is for *aesthetics*. Aesthetics is smell and taste. Every water filter out there is an aesthetics filter. If a filter didn't do a good job in the A category, then it wouldn't be a water filter. If water isn't improved in terms of taste and smell by a filter, then it's really not going to sell.

My experience has been 99.9 percent with clean, potable water—water from cities and towns that has been chlorinated and mostly fluoridated. There is a whole host of issues related to many, many places in the world that do not have access to clean drinking water. This section is not so much about them, but it is about those of us that are fortunate enough to have a faucet to turn on where the water comes out. While it may be not perfect in every way, at least it's potable.

When people get used to something—whatever it is—they will defend it. So, if somebody drinks water in a particular location, and you change that water, they are often going to give you a funny look or wrinkle their nose, and say: *Oh, I don't like this. This doesn't taste right* because they're used to something else. A different person might be accustomed to water in a different place, with a different taste. When it comes to the aesthetics of water—the smell and the taste—it's a subjective experience.

Biologics

The B in the ABCs of water filtration stands for *biologics*. Biologics are viruses, pathogens, and bacteria living in water. Until 1907, this was a big concern all over the world, so water chlorination began. As much as people don't like chlorine, adding chlorine to water eliminated the biologics category.

Not everyone has water where the biologics are addressed with chlorine, ozonation, or other technologies, so they do actually have a concern. If you're drinking from a mountain stream, if you have a broken water main in your community and they issue a boil order, or if you live in an area of the world that doesn't have chlorinated water, you need a B filter, a biologics filter.

If you're shopping for a traditional water filter, you want to search for this function. They're not going to be labeled, *B for biologics,* but you want to look for information about viruses, bacteria, and pathogens. If a filter reduces or removes those, that's what you're looking for.

Can a structured water device act as a B filter?

Scientifically, the answer is no. However, if we're talking about what makes a difference in people's lives, the answer depends on your personal experience. I've read testimonials and watched videos on the internet showing people using structured water technologies as biologic water treatment systems.

I was never comfortable making a recommendation to use a structured water device as a B system until I went to South America and went to a pueblo with water that is not chlorinated. I drank the water through a structured water device, and I didn't get sick. Now I'm not asking you to risk your vacation or your health based on my personal experience, but I am suggesting that you can experiment with this issue if you want. You may find a structured water device is sufficient.

I received reports from customers who have been to Mexico, India, and even the Amazon, and drunk water known to have viruses, bacteria, and parasites in it, and they were fine using the structured water device.

Chemicals

The C in the ABCs of water filtration stands for *chemicals*. One of the chemicals that people worry the most about in water is fluoride, and it's one that I have a good bit of experience with, so I'd like to share that with you.

The whole time that I've been in the structured water business, I've been living in a home that has municipal water that is fluoridated. I've only used a filter for a couple of months of those years. Fluoride concerns me because it can cause calcification of our pineal gland, but once it is altered with structured water, I am comfortable that it cannot harm me.

Over the years, I've had the opportunity to interact with a lot of alternative health providers and different people who use energetics to test things. I've asked many of them whether my body is sufficiently protected from chemicals by a structured water device. All those people have affirmed that my body is safe.

When you consider treating the C portion of water, a structured water device is definitely a viable technology to use. If you're uncomfortable using a structured water device, then I recommend using a traditional water filter. Pick one that has laboratory results to remove the toxins that are concerns in your area.

PUTTING YOUR ABCS INTO PRACTICE, PART II

Dissolved Solids

The D in the ABCs of water filtration is for dissolved solids, and these are the metals leached from old pipes. Most of the water infrastructure in our homes and under our roads is fairly old. When I was a member of my local water company's consumer advisory council, I learned that up to 44 percent of water that leaves water treatment plants in the United States never makes it to a home because there are so many leaks and cracks along the way. That tells you a little bit about the state of the pipes underground. Of course, the state of the pipes in your home depends on when they were installed and what material they are.

Typically, metals come from these pipes, and we call them dissolved solids. If you are looking for a solution for lead or copper, those products are widely available on water filter companies' websites. You can read them and their lab results, and it's pretty easy to match up with a lead-removing filter that meets your need.

If I lived in an old home or had some reason to think that the pipes around me were really decayed, then I would choose a sediment-blocking filter, which is available at home improvement stores and is fairly inexpensive. My preference is to place a sediment filter on the whole-house level as a complement to the structured water device. So, I would take care of the chemistry of water by blocking those larger sediment particulates at the whole-house level; then I would take care of energizing the water with a physics-based structuring device at the place where the water is consumed.

A lot of people think they should test water with a *total dissolved solids* (TDS) meter. It's not necessarily a great indicator because mineral content can contribute to a high TDS rating, and there's no reason to remove mineral content from water. They can actually be pollutants, but a TDS meter won't tell you which it is. I would drink structured water that has a TDS number of 200 or 300 because it would most likely be minerals or salts.

Energy

The E in the ABCs of water filtration is for energy. Now we are discussing the various physics-based devices. As the structured water movement is gaining momentum, there are a lot more technologies being offered in the marketplace. Because I've looked at as many of them as anybody, I receive a lot of inquiries about which one is best. So, let's go back to our transportation analogy here. First, if you're looking at a structured water technology, it's like putting yourself in a modern automobile instead of self-propelled transportation. In that context, you can't possibly do anything wrong.

Now, once you recognize that you're in the modern automobile, you want to choose the one that's best for you. Some criteria about structured water devices that you can evaluate include infinite energies and manmade energy. In the realm of infinite energies, I've experimented with sacred geometry, vortexing, and the mineral kingdom (crystals). They all resonate deeply with me. I've tested all of them with thousands of people, and I've seen them make a difference in people's lives.

In the structured water technologies that use manmade energies, a number of systems on the market use electricity, and they might act as a blender to spin water. Electricity impacts our water by introducing unnatural frequencies that are not harmonic with our energy fields. If we can stay away from these type of energies as much as possible, it supports our overall well-being.

In addition, a number of companies are using magnets, another structuring technology. The problem with magnets is they bring polarity to water. Polarity is black and white. Polarity is not oneness and love, so philosophically I do not want to use magnets, and I tend to redirect my efforts into alignment with the infinite energies.

No matter which system you choose, if you use a structured water device, you're moving to a higher level that's better for your consciousness and for your health. If you can choose those that resonate most with the energies of nature, you'll be the most supported.

You can never go wrong with a structured water device. They add harmony to everything. They work well with everything and using them with any other system doesn't in any way degrade the other system. Structured water devices bring infinite energies to your water.

When you choose infinite energies to influence your water, you allow the water to revitalize itself. When that water enters your body, it is easier to for your cells to use, and it connects to the unified field, to Source, to oneness. That connection brings benefits to the body, mind, and spirit.

FREQUENTLY ASKED QUESTIONS

What if I'm afraid of fluoride and chlorine?

When my structured water business first became successful, I began to field phone calls from people all over the world. It was startling to me to notice that in the same week a customer from Africa had the same concerns as a customer from Australia and a customer from the United States. I began to understand how connected everything is, and how easy it is for cultures to manipulate people and cause them to think the same way and have the same concerns.

Listen to the setup.

The question people most often call with is: *How do I remove fluoride or chlorine from my water?*

Those are the two things that our water companies are intentionally putting in the water. It's absurd! It's unbelievable: The things that people want *out* of the water are the very things that the government, the structure, and the system are putting into the water.

So, if you have concerns about fluoride and chlorine, there are two ways to go. If you need to remove it, then use a chemistry-based filter. If you're comfortable transforming it and neutralizing the toxins, which means they will not be physically removed but they will be energetically neutralized, then use a physics-based structuring device. It's okay to use both.

What if my budget is really tight?

When I entered this business, I entered from the perspective of service, rather than seeing how much money I could make. Still, as I described to you in the *Run Away* section earlier, when I learned that physics-based structuring devices don't have any replacement parts, I ran away from it for a while. I knew it was a really bad business to be in from a financial perspective if I was selling products that didn't have replacement parts. It's just not how businesses are created these days.

However, when you want to do sacred commerce with people, and you want to change the world, you must be willing to do things differently. Even though it didn't look good from an economic perspective, I took the plunge into a business where you could buy a device manufactured to last a lifetime.

If your budget is tight, I recommend taking advantage of the properties of physics-based water structuring devices. First, they're generally sold with money-back guarantees, so you can try one on a risk-free basis. If you end up liking it, then you have bought something that was engineered to last a long time and not have any additional cost. This is a great place to start.

If, after using a physics-based device for a while, you determine that you are still uncomfortable with some aspect of your water, then you can add a chemistry-based filter. Because you will already have the structuring device in place, you'll probably be more likely to buy a less expensive filter and to trust it more.

What if I can afford anything I want?

For some of us, money isn't an issue. Whether we spend a couple thousand extra dollars on our credit card in a given month has no bearing on how we feel about ourselves or our stress. If that describes you, you can make your decision based upon your preferences without regard to money.

In that case, my advice is to begin with a whole-house water structuring device. Change the energy of water in every aspect of your home—from the hot water heater that's probably in your basement or garage, to the appliances throughout your house, to every plant, animal, and human in your home—and the drinking water. Essentially, every time you move a faucet, you'll be moving harmonious energy through your water.

Experience that first, and let it flow for thirty to sixty days so that the energy field builds up. If you achieve satisfaction with that, you're done. Just because you have a lot of money doesn't mean you need to waste it, and if a solution that works and satisfies you doesn't have any replacement parts, that's a good thing. If after thirty to sixty days, you find yourself still uncomfortable with any aspect of the new science of transforming the toxins of water, then you can simply add a chemistry-based filter. You can choose to do that at the whole-house level or at the point-of-use level by choosing something for your kitchen sink or shower.

What if I live in an apartment or in a house?

You may choose a whole-house filter, an under-sink filter, or a shower filter. Structuring devices include whole-house, under-sink, shower, and garden devices, as well as portable devices.

My suggestion is to *not* select purchases the way I did! I first bought a structured shower device, then a portable unit, then a sink device, and *then* a whole-house structuring unit. I spent more on these devices than was necessary as I now simply use my whole-house unit for nearly everything!

If you own a home, I suggest purchasing a whole-house device and to buy a portable device as well. Once you are accustomed to using structured water at home and immersing your life in it, you're not going to want to be without it. You can take the portable device with you when traveling to continue enjoying the benefits of structured water when on the road and abroad.

If you live in an apartment, you will probably want to use point-of-use devices. These are easier to install than whole-house devices, and they don't require the cutting of a pipe. Since people tend to think of cutting a pipe as being a more permanent installation, I recommend you consider a shower device that goes right on your shower, a sink device that goes under your sink, and a garden device if you have access to a garden. Of course, a portable device is great for everyone.

What if I have a well?

Wells are interesting because they're always different. Every person I've spoken to about wells has slight variations in their situation. Generally, there is knowledge in your local community about how to treat well water through chemistry, and that local knowledge won't include any aspects pertaining to the benefits of structuring.

Tap into the local knowledge about how people filter their water.

Ask this question: Do the wells in this area have a lot of sediment in them, so they tend to produce substantial particulates in the water?

If that's the case, you'll most likely need a significantly sized tank and chemistry-based traditional water filter system right at your point of entry. Once the water has gone through a system like that to greatly reduce the mineral content in the water, and possibly to balance the pH, then you can consider a structured water device.

The recommendation I make to people with a well is to put a whole-house structuring device after a chemistry-based filter, or to put point-of-use systems at your sink and shower. Structured water devices do work harmoniously with softeners, so if you feel the need for a softener, you can use a structuring device too. Some people find that a structuring device is sufficient for softening and can replace a softener. So, before you invest in a softener, you might want to put a structuring device in first to see if your hard water problems are solved.

What if I believe in oneness?

This section is dedicated to those who believe that everything is an energetic experience.

You may have life experiences that helped open you to these possibilities:

- Everything is connected.
- Everything is here to serve you.

People often contact me while they're still grappling with deepening and anchoring those beliefs into their being. If that's you, you probably know it.

Physics-based, structured water devices are a tool for those on an awakening path, a journey of oneness. They reconnect the spirituality of water with each human being. If you find yourself on this journey, know that even if it feels like a leap of faith to use structuring technology as your choice, it is the right choice. This rightness is why structured water devices are popular, because so many of us are awakening.

We want to know: Which water does an awakening being choose?

You don't have to be confused about water anymore. You can apply the principles in this book. You can have confidence. We are now in the Age of Aquarius, and with it, the mysteries of water are unraveling. With recent science from people like Dr. Emoto and Dr. Pollack, we're scratching the surface and beginning to understand the many mysteries of water.

There are still many other mysteries to unfold. As you join us in immersing yourself in living water, you will be supported in your journey of re-discovering your multi-dimensional self. You will experience how structured water leads to an understanding that it is a living consciousness that's here to help you remember the state of oneness. As you awaken to your own truth, clarify your beliefs, and grow solid in your knowing of who you are, you'll be able to contribute your authentic voice to our species and way of life.

We are a species under siege. If each of us takes the opportunity to become the greatest versions of ourselves, then collectively, we can discover what is possible for us as a species. I invite you to discover the mysteries of water with us and to contribute your voice as a multi-dimensional being.

> *Structured water is like a shower for my soul.*
> ~ Christian M.

Conclusion

I have always loved games of strategy since I was young, and my competitive father who taught me backgammon at age five or six, started getting quite frustrated with me when I began beating him about 90 percent of the time. While I didn't understand it at the time, looking back I can now see that I like to figure out the rules and how things work, and then to dive deeply into understanding such structures and systems. That's exactly what I did with backgammon.

When I was eight, there was a tennis pro at our club who was quite cocky. My dad set me up in a backgammon match against him, and then he encouraged a bunch of people to watch. I think the crowd was about fifteen or twenty people when we sat down for our game. When we got to our last roll, he hadn't taken a piece off yet, and people wondered if I was going to roll doubles and take all my pieces off before he got one off the board.

I called out loud for double fours so that the audience could hear me and rolled those dice. I'll be darned if double fours didn't pop up to a roar from the crowd. I've always played games by first knowing the rules, but then there's a second layer. When I was little, I would have called it luck, and as I got older, I called it intuition. Now, I would call it connecting with the universal force.

As I got older, my game-playing turned to the stock market. I figured it was so diverse and complex that I would never be able to fully master it. But I was able to whittle it down to two factors. I would hypnotize or mesmerize myself every night by studying the price and number of shares traded for individual stocks. When I compared them on charts, I could make intuitive decisions about which stocks were going to move up. I did so with great success.

Now, I've shifted my game from the stock market to: *How does life work?*

I really want to know how life works, and I consider myself a game piece in the game of life. I want to play my piece in alignment with the rules of how life works. What I figured out is that it's a vibrational universe, and everything is energy.

Those energies are either harmonious, or they're chaotic, and the chaotic energies know this. They've cloaked their agenda well. They've got us living in a world where we're so busy that we don't have time to connect with ourselves or nature, and we're living lives that are producing tons of toxins. We're forcing systems on people that are so oppressive our youth are entering schools with guns and killing one another. Acts of terror make the news daily. These are symptoms of this chaotic energy throughout our world.

If we want to create change in the world, we have an opportunity to see through the rules of the game and understand that everything is vibration—that everything is energy.

We must recognize chaotic energies like these:

- Alcohol
- Addictive substances
- Violent video games, TV shows, and movies
- Oppressive systems

And align ourselves with harmonizing energies like these:

- Walks in nature
- Laughter with friends
- Living water

I call these *life essence technologies* (LET). When I build more life essence technologies into my life, I create more harmony, I know who I am, and I contribute more of myself to life.

Now that you've had the opportunity to read this book, consider that your solution for water is more than a filter. Think about it as an opportunity for awakening yourself. Water is energy, and water is the catalyst carrying messages of oneness that help us wake up to lives of love and joy. If we can rediscover that living water in our lives, we may just be able to alter the future of humanity.

I invite and encourage you to take three actions:

1. **Don't buy plastic water bottles.** Don't do it. Stop now! Figure out how to manage your circumstances

so that you don't buy any more. I used to think there were exceptions, and that I still had to buy bottles sometimes. It's been quite a while now since I've bought one. I've had times where I've gone more than a year or two consecutively without a single bottle. If I can do it, so can you.

2. **Choose harmony.** Become educated about this vibrational universe and decide: *Do I want to create harmony in my life?* If so, consider doing that with the very building blocks you're created from—the water you're made of.

3. **Listen for your life's purpose.** It's about more than being comfortable. We're conditioned by the chaotic energies to want lives in which we think it's enough to make money for ourselves and our families. It's not very fulfilling. It's true that money can't buy happiness. Consider the circumstances of your life from the perspective of fulfilling your contribution to the human species.

My purpose is to help people understand the energy of water.

What's yours?

Next Steps

Fueled by unrelenting passion, Patrick is on a mission to up-lift humanity by creating a world of Love and Oneness. He will support you as you awaken your superpowers through immersion in living water, quantum physics, and loving all that is.

To find out more about Patrick and the magic of being immersed in living water, visit TheWellnessEnterprise.com.

There are lots of additional resources to support you, including courses, specials, sales, and recommended reading.

About the Author

As a financial advisor for eighteen years, Patrick Durkin learned that success with money doesn't equal a satisfying life. Called to make a difference for people and the planet, he left his first career to found The Wellness Enterprise, Inc. to create a solution to the plastic water bottle problem.

Researching traditional filters, Patrick learned about the chemistry of water and then the physics of water through structured water devices. He experienced how sacred geometry, vortexing, and precious gems can naturally revitalize, energize, and purify water. He created *Water Magic 101*, a course designed to help others understand these phenomena. He also markets water solutions through a global network of alternative health providers.

As a public speaker, Patrick has supported tens of thousands of people to understand and benefit from structured water. He's been interviewed by dozens of health- and spirituality-focused telesummit, radio, and podcast hosts. Darius

Barazandeh, from *You Wealth Revolution*, calls Patrick "the voice of water."

A perpetual student of personal development, Patrick has an unrelenting passion for understanding how life works and what humanity can do to restore harmony in the world. He's an avid gardener and hiker. His favorite pastime is walking on the rocks near the ocean with his four kids.

www.ingramcontent.com/pod-product-compliance
Lightning Source LLC
Chambersburg PA
CBHW050536280326
41933CB00011B/1607